THE BOY WHO CRIED WOLF

NARRATED BY THE

SHEEPISH BUT TRUTHFUL WOLF

BY NANCY LOEWEN

ILLUSTRATED BY
JUAN M. MORENO

PICTURE WINDOW BOOKS
a capstone imprint

Editor: Jill Kalz
Designer: Lori Bye
Premedia Specialist: Kris Wilfahrt
The illustrations in this book were created digitally.
Design Element: Shutterstock, Andrey_Kuzman

⁓☙✤☙⁓

Picture Window Books
1710 Roe Crest Drive
North Mankato, MN 56003
www.mycapstone.com

Library of Congress Cataloging-in-Publication Data
Names: Loewen, Nancy, 1964– author. |
Moreno, Juan Manuel, 1972– illustrator.
Title: The boy who cried wolf, narrated by the sheepish but truthful wolf /
by Nancy Loewen ; illustrated by Juan M. Moreno.
Description: North Mankato, Minnesota : Picture Window Books, [2018] |
Series: Nonfiction picture books. The other side of the fable |
Summary: In this humorous retelling of the classic fable, Whisper the wolf
explains that the shepherd boy was not lying about there being a wolf among
the sheep, he just misunderstood the situation, because Whisper was just
visiting the sheep who were his friends.
Identifiers: LCCN 2018005705 (print) | LCCN 2018006556 (ebook) |
ISBN 9781515828778 (eBook PDF) | ISBN 9781515828693 (library binding) |
ISBN 9781515828730 (paperback)
Subjects: LCSH: Fables. | Sheep—Juvenile fiction. | Wolves—Juvenile
fiction. | Truthfulness and falsehood—Juvenile fiction. | Humorous stories.
| CYAC: Fables. | Sheep—Fiction. | Wolves—Fiction. | Honesty—Fiction. |
Humorous stories. | LCGFT: Fables. | Humorous fiction.
Classification: LCC PZ8.2.L63 (ebook) | LCC PZ8.2.L63 Bo 2018 (print) |
DDC [E]—dc23
LC record available at https://lccn.loc.gov/2018005705

Printed in the United States.
PA021

A fable is a short animal tale that teaches a lesson. It is one of the oldest story forms. "The Boy Who Cried Wolf" is from a collection of hundreds of fables called *Aesop's Fables*. These stories may have been written by Aesop, a Greek storyteller who lived from 620 to 560 BC.

A shepherd boy became bored while caring for his master's flock of sheep. So he thought of a plan to amuse himself.

He ran toward the village. "Wolf! Wolf!" he cried. As he expected, the villagers dropped what they were doing and rushed to the pasture. But there was no wolf—only the boy, laughing and laughing about the trick he'd played.

A few days later, the boy again shouted, "Wolf! Wolf!" The villagers ran to help, only to find they'd been tricked once more.

Then one night a wolf really *did* attack the sheep. The boy was terrified. "Wolf! Wolf!" he cried.

But this time no one came to help.

The moral of the story:

Liars aren't believed, even when they tell the truth.

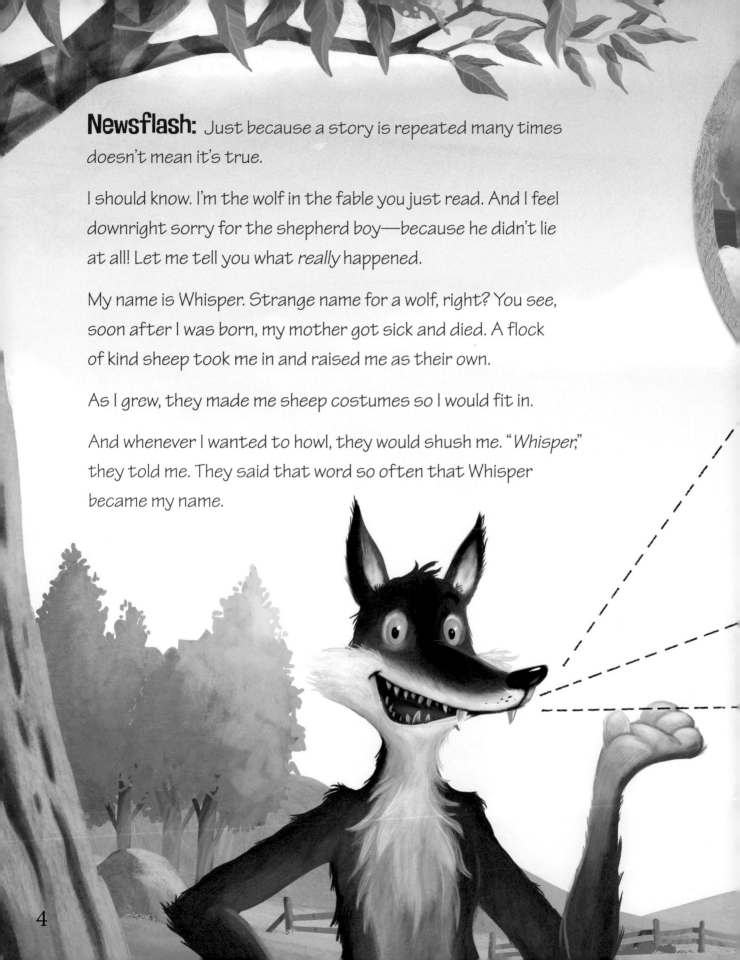

Newsflash: Just because a story is repeated many times doesn't mean it's true.

I should know. I'm the wolf in the fable you just read. And I feel downright sorry for the shepherd boy—because he didn't lie at all! Let me tell you what *really* happened.

My name is Whisper. Strange name for a wolf, right? You see, soon after I was born, my mother got sick and died. A flock of kind sheep took me in and raised me as their own.

As I grew, they made me sheep costumes so I would fit in.

And whenever I wanted to howl, they would shush me. "*Whisper,*" they told me. They said that word so often that Whisper became my name.

4

I loved my sheep family, but I couldn't live with them forever. A wolf is meant to roam. So, when I was all grown up, I said goodbye and set out on all sorts of wolf adventures.

I took up cross-country running ...

tried lots of new foods ...

made friends with three little pigs (but that's a whole other story) ...

I even joined a choir.

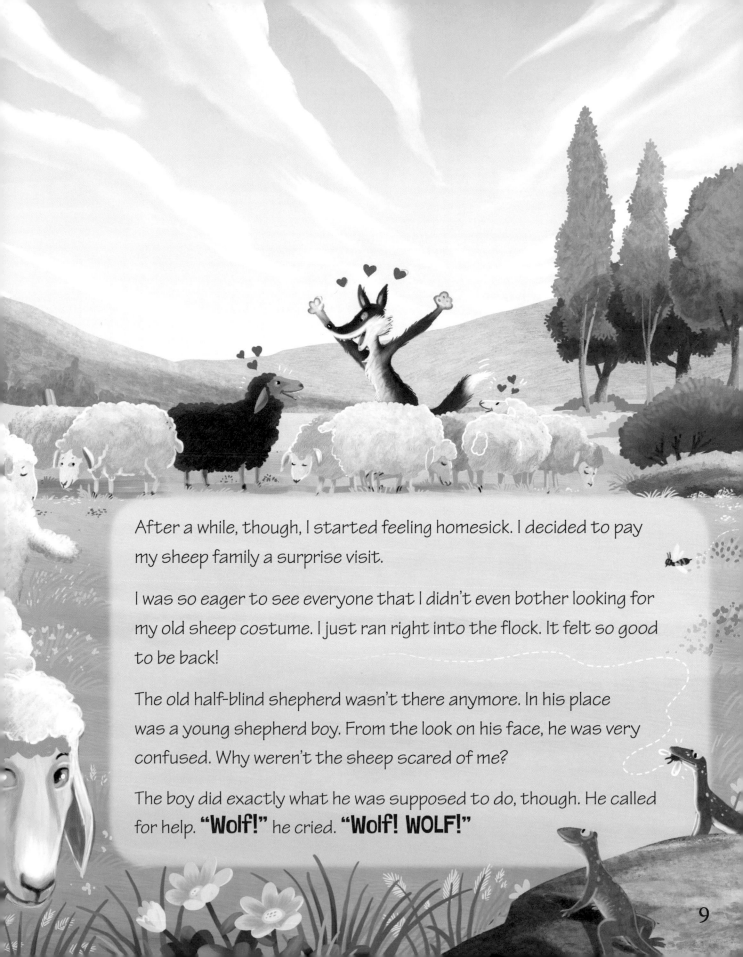

After a while, though, I started feeling homesick. I decided to pay my sheep family a surprise visit.

I was so eager to see everyone that I didn't even bother looking for my old sheep costume. I just ran right into the flock. It felt so good to be back!

The old half-blind shepherd wasn't there anymore. In his place was a young shepherd boy. From the look on his face, he was very confused. Why weren't the sheep scared of me?

The boy did exactly what he was supposed to do, though. He called for help. **"Wolf!"** he cried. **"Wolf! WOLF!"**

I scrambled to a hiding spot behind a large tree and watched as the villagers came racing to the pasture. They were yelling like crazy.

Then they stopped short.

There was no wolf. And the sheep were calm.

"Is this some kind of trick?" demanded the flock's owner. His name was Walter.

"There *was*—a—wolf!" The boy was so upset that he couldn't catch his breath. He started wheezing. "No—trick! I really— saw—a wolf!" he gasped.

Some of the villagers standing farthest away from the boy mistook the wheezing for giggling. "What, is he *laughing?*" they asked. "Does he think this is a joke?"

I wanted to roll my eyes. Humans have terrible hearing. Absolutely terrible.

The next time I visited the flock, I was more careful. I squeezed into my old sheep costume first. But—well, this is embarrassing—but after only a few hugs, that stretched-out costume popped right off.

The shepherd boy spotted me immediately. Once more his training kicked in.

"Wolf! Wolf—WOLF!" he shouted.

Again, the villagers stormed the pasture. The boy wheezed and gasped. And the villagers in the rear grumbled about the boy laughing.

The next day, I noticed something very strange. I pricked up my ears and squinted hard.

Walter and the villagers were putting my friend Baaarbara into a wolf costume!

Well, I'm no dummy. I knew they were trying to scare the boy and teach him a lesson.

Baaarbara darted here and there among the sheep.

For the third time, the shepherd boy cried, "Wolf! WOLF! WOLF!"

Of course, no one came to help.

But the boy was braver than anyone knew. He grabbed a club and went after poor little Baaarbara!

I had to save my friend. And Walter had to save his sheep.

We both ran to Baaarbara at the same moment.

Time seemed to stop. We all stared at each other—the boy, Walter, Baaarbara, the villagers, the sheep, and me.

Suddenly the boy threw down his club. "I QUIT!" he shouted. "I quit, I quit, I QUIT! I thought being a shepherd would be easy. But none of this makes any sense. I'm going back to Pet Grooming School!"

Walter didn't have a shepherd anymore. What he *did* have was a wonderful idea . . .

And that's how my sheep family and I ended up in Wooly Walt's Traveling Sheep and Wolf Show. Now we ALL get to see the world.

Back to that moral about liars not being believed . . . It makes perfect sense—it just doesn't fit here. I say, whether you're a wolf in sheep's clothing, a sheep in wolf's clothing, or anything in between, remember:

There's always more to the story than meets the eye!

THINK ABOUT IT

Describe at least three ways in which Whisper's version of the fable is different from the original fable.

Explain how this story would change if it were told from another character's point of view, such as the shepherd boy. How about Walter? Or Baaarbara?

Describe a time when you met someone who turned out to be much different than you first thought—in a good or bad way.

GLOSSARY

Aesop (AY-sop)—a Greek storyteller (620–560 BC) whose fables teach a lesson

character—a person, animal, or creature in a story

confused—uncertain about something

fable—a short animal tale that teaches a lesson

moral—a lesson about what is right and wrong

pasture—land where farm animals eat grass and exercise

point of view—a way of looking at something

shepherd—a person who takes care of sheep

terrified—very scared

version—an account of something from a certain point of view

READ MORE

Hoena, Blake, retold by. *The Boy Who Cried Wolf.* Classic Fables in Rhythm and Rhyme. North Mankato, Minn.: Cantata Learning, 2018.

Magoon, Scott. *The Boy Who Cried Bigfoot!* New York: Simon & Schuster Books for Young Readers, 2013.

Miller, Connie Colwell. *Andrew and the Birthday Surprise: The Boy Who Cried Wolf Remixed.* Aesop's Fables Remixed. Mankato, Minn.: Amicus Illustrated, 2017.

INTERNET SITES

Use FactHound to find Internet sites related to this book.

Visit *www.facthound.com*

Just type in 9781515828693 and go.

LOOK FOR ALL THE BOOKS IN THE SERIES:

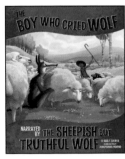
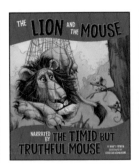